Exploring History through Simple Recipes

Oregon Trail Cooking

by Mary Gunderson

Consultant: Robert L. Munkres, Professor Emeritus,
Muskingum College, New Concord, Ohio,
Author of *Saleratus and Sagebrush: The Oregon Trail through Wyoming*

Blue Earth Books

an imprint of Capstone Press
Mankato, Minnesota

Blue Earth Books are published by Capstone Press
151 Good Counsel Drive, P.O. Box 669, Mankato, Minnesota 56002
http://www.capstone-press.com

Library of Congress Cataloging-in-Publication Data
Gunderson, Mary.
    Oregon Trail cooking / by Mary Gunderson.
    p. cm.—(Exploring history through simple recipes)
    Includes bibliographical references (p. 30) and index.
    Summary: Discusses the everyday life, family roles, cooking methods, and common foods of pioneers who traveled west on the Oregon Trail during the nineteenth century. Includes recipes.
    ISBN 0-7368-0355-6
    1. Cookery, American—Western style—History Juvenile literature. 2. Food habits—Oregon Trail—History—19th century Juvenile literature. 3. Frontier and pioneer life—Oregon Trail Juvenile literature. [1. Cookery, American—Western style—History. 2. Food habits—West (U.S.)—History—19th century. 3. Frontier and pioneer life—West (U.S.). 4. Oregon Trail.] I. Title. II. Series.
TX715.2.W47G88 2000
394.1'0978'09034—dc21   99-27054
                                                                            CIP

Editorial credits
Editor, Rachel Koestler; cover designer, Steve Christensen; interior designer, Heather Kindseth; illustrator, Linda Clavel; photo researcher, Kimberly Danger.

Acknowledgments
Blue Earth Books thanks the following children who helped test recipes: John Christensen, Matthew Christensen, Maerin Coughlan, Beth Goebel, Nicole Hilger, Abby Rothenbuehler, Alice Ruff, Hannah Schoof, and Molly Wandersee.

Photo credits
Corbis/Bettmann, cover; Gregg Andersen, cover (background), and recipes, 14, 18, 21, 23, 29; Wyoming Division of Cultural Resources, 6; FPG International LLC, 8, 22; Archive Photos, 9; North Wind Picture Archives, 10, 16, 19; Kansas State Historical Society, 13; Photo Network, 17, 26; Montana Historical Society, 20-21; Utah State Historical Society, 24; Photo Network, 28; Corcoran Gallery of Art, 12

Editor's note
Adult supervision may be needed for some recipes in this book. All recipes have been tested. Although based on historical foods, recipes have been modernized and simplified for today's young cooks.

1 2 3 4 5 6 05 04 03 02 01 00

Contents

Cooking Help

Recipes

References

Metric Conversion Guide

U.S.	Canada
¼ teaspoon	1 mL
½ teaspoon	2 mL
1 teaspoon	5 mL
1 tablespoon	15 mL
¼ cup	50 mL
⅓ cup	75 mL
½ cup	125 mL
⅔ cup	150 mL
¾ cup	175 mL
1 cup	250 mL
1 quart	1 liter
1 ounce	30 grams
2 ounces	55 grams
4 ounces	85 grams
½ pound	225 grams
1 pound	455 grams

Fahrenheit	Celsius
325 degrees	160 degrees
350 degrees	180 degrees
375 degrees	190 degrees
400 degrees	200 degrees
425 degrees	220 degrees

Kitchen Safety

1. Make sure your hair and clothes will not be in the way while you are cooking.

2. Keep a fire extinguisher in the kitchen. Never put water on a grease fire.

3. Wash your hands with soap before you start to cook. Wash your hands with soap again after you handle meat or poultry.

4. Ask an adult for help with sharp knives, the stove, the oven, and all electrical appliances.

5. Turn handles of pots and pans to the middle of the stove. A person walking by could run into handles that stick out toward the room.

6. Use dry pot holders to take dishes out of the oven.

7. Wash all fruits and vegetables.

8. Always use a clean cutting board. Wash the cutting board thoroughly after cutting meat or poultry.

9. Wipe up spills immediately.

10. Store leftovers properly. Do not leave leftovers out at room temperature for more than two hours.

Cooking Equipment

mixing bowls

liquid measuring cup

coffee cans

baking pans

sharp knife

cutting board

pot holder

measuring spoons

wire cooling rack

duct tape

dry-ingredient measuring cups

rolling pin

Dutch oven

pitcher

wooden spoon

vegetable peeler

pastry blender

slotted spoon

colander

spoon

spatula

large skillet

jar

large saucepan

wire mesh strainer

medium skillet

strainer

medium saucepan

The Oregon Trail

In the mid-1800s, many people journeyed across the western United States on the Oregon Trail. This route stretched across more than 2,000 miles (3,200 kilometers) of unsettled land. People who traveled to the new land were called emigrants. Emigrants also were called overlanders because they traveled such a great distance. Many emigrants were farmers who were eager to build homes and plant crops on the inexpensive or free land of the West.

Overlanders began their journey on the Oregon Trail in the spring from towns along the Missouri River. They loaded their wagons onto steamboats. The steamboats then brought travelers up the Missouri River to towns near the start of Oregon Trail. The towns where the steamboats stopped were called jumping-off towns. Steamboats dropped off pioneers and their belongings at these stops.

From jumping-off towns, emigrants traveled to the western territories of Oregon, California, or Utah. For about two-thirds of the way, all travelers used the same trail. The trail then split and led to the different territories. Many farmers headed for the Oregon Territory. Later, this territory became the states of Washington, Oregon, and Idaho.

Wagon wheels left deep ruts in the prairie. One wagon after another traveled in the same ruts. On many areas of the Oregon Trail, these ruts still can be seen today.

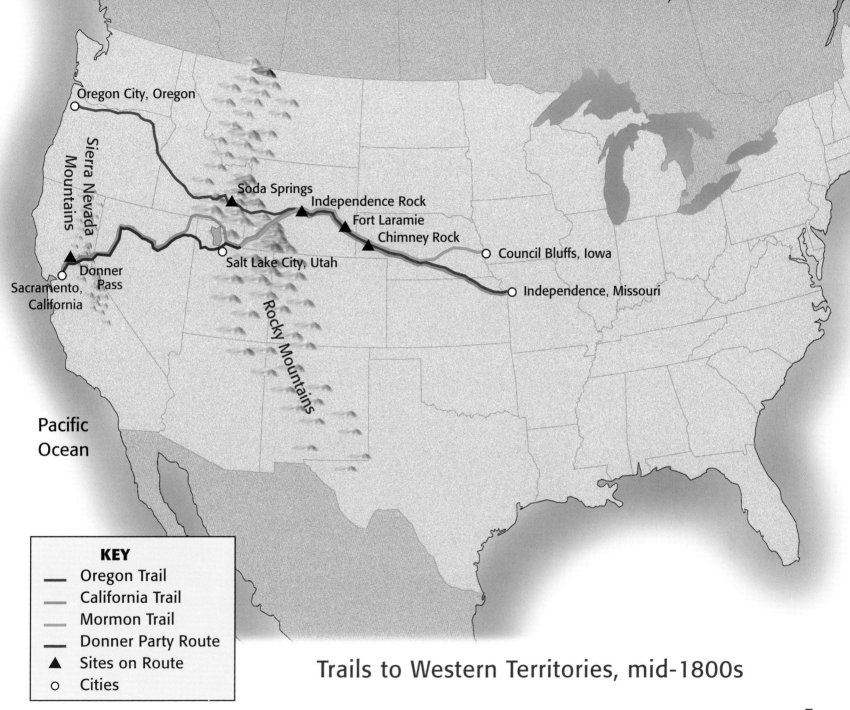

Oregon City, Oregon

Sierra Nevada Mountains

Soda Springs

Independence Rock

Fort Laramie

Chimney Rock

Council Bluffs, Iowa

Salt Lake City, Utah

Donner Pass

Sacramento, California

Independence, Missouri

Rocky Mountains

Pacific Ocean

KEY
— Oregon Trail
— California Trail
— Mormon Trail
— Donner Party Route
▲ Sites on Route
○ Cities

Trails to Western Territories, mid-1800s

Emigrants moved west in covered wagons called prairie schooners. A schooner is a type of sailboat. From a distance, the white wagon covers looked like sails blowing across the prairie grass. Some families wrote their names and hometowns on the canvas cover. Others drew pictures of eagles, oxen, or elephants. Some people wrote messages on the wagon cover such as "Never Say Die."

From jumping-off towns, the trip west took about four to five months to complete. A full day's journey was an average of 10 to 15 miles (16 to 24 kilometers). The only person who rode in the prairie schooner was the driver. Other family members walked alongside it. Less weight inside the wagon reduced the strain on oxen and mules.

The wagon rocked back and forth on the bumpy trail. Sitting in the wagon was an uncomfortable ride. On rainy days, emigrants traveled inside the wagon. Many overlanders became seasick from the rocking motion. Some travelers hung jars of cream inside the wagon. During the day, the bumpy trail rocked the jar and churned the cream into butter.

Prairie schooners were about 10 feet (3 meters) long and 4 feet (1.2 meters) wide. Overlanders packed as many possessions as they could fit into the wagon. They often packed fragile items such as glass or china in a barrel of cornmeal.

Wagon Trains

Traveling alone on the Oregon Trail was dangerous. Groups of emigrants formed wagon trains for protection. An average wagon train consisted of 15 to 25 wagons. Before they left, the travelers elected a trail master and set up rules for the journey.

Members of a wagon train depended upon each other. They shared food and supplies with one another. They divided up chores and other work to help members of the wagon train survive. If the parents of a family died, the remaining members of the wagon train took care of the orphans.

Wagon trains did not always stay together. Members sometimes argued about rules and could not come to an agreement. When disagreements happened, the wagon train often split up. The new wagon train would elect a trail master and continue west.

Wagon Packing

Wagons pulled by oxen or mules carried all of the travelers' belongings. Wagons could hold up to 2,000 pounds (900 kilograms) of food and supplies. The average cost of a wagon, food, and supplies was $1,500.

Travelers did not have any way to keep their food cold. Fresh meat and vegetables spoiled quickly. Instead of large amounts of fresh foods, travelers chose dry goods that would keep for several months. Typical supplies included flour, cornmeal, bacon, coffee, sugar, and salt. In addition to these items, travelers packed rice, dried beans, and dried fruit. Guidebooks advised overlanders on how many pounds of each food to pack.

Keeping food dry was important for the travelers. If food became damp, worms or maggots infested it. Emigrants brushed the canvas wagon cover with linseed oil to keep the wagon contents dry. Linseed oil kept water from soaking through the cover and damaging food and other supplies.

Emigrants packed basic cooking utensils such as cast iron pots, butter churns, knives, tin plates, and forks. The travelers also brought hunting and fishing equipment. Emigrants strapped extra wagon wheels, gardening tools, chairs, and lanterns along the sides of the prairie schooner and underneath the wagon box.

Some travelers packed a bed. But there was not enough room for an entire family to sleep inside the schooner. Some emigrants brought tents. Most people slept outside on the ground. On rainy nights, they spread a piece of canvas underneath the wagon box. The canvas protected them from the wet ground. The wagon box served as a shelter to keep the emigrants dry during the night.

Emigrants paid about $1,500 for a prairie schooner and supplies. This amount was a high price in the mid-1800s. Many overlanders were wealthy. Those who could not afford the trip hired themselves out as wagon drivers.

Dutch Ovens

One of the most valued cooking pots on the Oregon Trail was the Dutch oven. A Dutch oven was a cast iron pot with a lid. An empty Dutch oven weighed up to 30 pounds (about 14 kilograms). Each pot was about 4 inches (10 centimeters) deep and had three or four stubby legs. The pot was almost impossible to chip, crack, or break. Dutch ovens were named after the Pennsylvania Dutch people, who used the pots to cook soups and stews.

Overlanders used the Dutch oven for many kinds of meals. The tight-fitting lid held in steam for cooking beans, meat, and vegetables. Cooks turned the lid upside down over the fire to grill food. Overlanders lined hot coals across the top of the lid to use the pot as a baking oven.

Boiled Potatoes and Peas

Ingredients	Equipment	
3 large potatoes	vegetable peeler	slotted spoon
4 slices bacon	sharp knife	measuring spoons
1 cup frozen peas, thawed	cutting board	measuring cups
¾ teaspoon dried dillweed	Dutch oven or a large saucepan	spatula
⅛ teaspoon salt	skillet	wooden spoon
⅛ teaspoon pepper	paper towel	
	clean coffee can	

1. Peel 3 potatoes. Cut potatoes in half lengthwise.
2. Place potatoes in Dutch oven or large saucepan. Add enough water to cover potatoes. Bring to boil.
3. Reduce heat to medium. Cook 20 minutes or until potatoes are nearly tender.
4. While potatoes are cooking, cut 4 slices bacon into 1-inch (2.5-centimeter) pieces.
5. In skillet, fry bacon until crisp. Place bacon on paper towel to cool.
6. Pour bacon fat into a coffee can. Scoop 2 tablespoons of fat out of the can and pour into the skillet.
7. Remove potatoes from water. Cool 10 minutes.
8. Cut potatoes into ¼-inch (.6-centimeter) slices.
9. Add sliced potatoes and 1 cup peas to skillet. Cook over medium heat. Gently turn after about 4 minutes. Cook 4 to 6 minutes longer or until hot.
10. Stir in bacon pieces, ¾ teaspoon dillweed, ⅛ teaspoon salt, and ⅛ teaspoon pepper. Cook 2 minutes.

Makes 6 to 8 servings

Mealtime: Morning, Noon, and Night

Emigrants cooked meals over an open fire. They set up two Y-shaped poles called crotches on either side of the fire. Overlanders secured a pole on the crotches. They hung pots and kettles on the pole. Other cast iron pots sat directly in the fire coals. On rainy days, it was difficult to keep the fire going. At these times, emigrants sometimes skipped meals or ate dried fruit and cold mush made from cornmeal and water.

Overlanders began their day by building up the fire from the previous night. They boiled water for coffee and fried bacon. Emigrants sometimes left a pot of beans simmering on the fire overnight. By morning, the beans were ready to eat. Breakfast often included dry bread or stiff crackers called hardtack. Some emigrants softened hardtack by frying it in lard or water.

Emigrants often ate leftovers for the noon meal. They dished up cold beans with bacon or dried buffalo meat. At supper, overlanders boiled rice, fried cornmeal biscuits, and made tea or coffee. They served dried beef or codfish with the rice. To make the meat soft, emigrants sometimes soaked it in water and stewed it with dried vegetables.

Emigrants gathered dried buffalo chips to fuel their fires. Three bushels of buffalo chips burned long enough to heat a meal.

When the wagon train "laid by" for a day or two, overlanders prepared bread dough and did some baking. They enjoyed the fresh biscuits and breads. But the yeast needed to bake bread was limited. Emigrants wanted to save as much yeast as they could to last throughout the trip. Near Independence Rock, the halfway point of their trip, some emigrants found sheets of saleratus on the ground. This saltlike powder could be used as a yeast to make bread rise. Many overlanders fried biscuits or cornmeal pancakes instead of baking bread.

Nooning

Travelers looked forward to "nooning," or stopping for the noon hour. They used this time to rest and have something to eat. Parents allowed their young children to run and play, and older children visited their friends in other wagons. Some children carried cloth bags to collect buffalo chips for the evening fire. Many overlanders used "nooning" time to write in their diaries and journals.

Animals needed nooning to drink water, graze, and rest up for the afternoon journey. Travelers wanted their animals to stay healthy. They did not want to overwork their oxen and mules. These animals were almost impossible to replace if they became sick or died. The trail master often picked a nooning spot that was best for the animals.

Salt-rising Bread

Emigrants sometimes made salt-rising bread. This recipe takes two days to complete.

DAY ONE

Ingredients
2½ cups warm water, 110°F to 115°F
   (43°C to 46°C)
1 package active dry yeast
   (2¼ teaspoons)
1½ teaspoons salt
1 teaspoon sugar
2 cups all-purpose flour

Equipment
large plastic bowl
liquid measuring cup
measuring spoons
dry-ingredient measuring cups
wooden spoon
plastic wrap
clean dish towel

1. In large plastic bowl, combine 2½ cups warm water,
   1 package yeast, 1½ teaspoons salt, and
   1 teaspoon sugar.
2. Stir in 2 cups flour. Beat well with a wooden
   spoon.
3. Cover bowl loosely with plastic wrap, then a
   towel. Let stand at room temperature for
   12 to 18 hours, stirring once or twice.

DAY TWO

Ingredients
4 cups all-purpose flour
½ cup flour for kneading
3 tablespoons butter or margarine
   for greasing

Equipment
large cutting board or large
   sheet of wax paper
large plastic bowls
3 paper towels or napkins

2 loaf pans, 9 inches by 5 inches
(23 centimeters by 13 centimeters)
pot holders
wire baking rack

---

1. Add 4 cups flour to dough mixture. Stir until dough becomes thick.
2. Lightly flour cutting board or a countertop lined with wax paper.
3. Turn dough out of bowl onto floured surface. Sprinkle enough flour on top of the dough to lightly cover the surface. Knead by pushing the dough with the heels of your palm, fold, and repeat. Knead for 7 to 10 minutes or until dough is smooth and stretchy. Add flour if dough sticks to your hand.
4. Use a paper towel or napkin dabbed with butter or margarine to grease second bowl. Continue dabbing butter and spreading over inside of bowl until lightly coated.
5. Place dough in bowl. Roll around to moisten surface of dough.
6. Cover with towel and set in a warm place to rise. Let rise 50 to 60 minutes or until doubled in size. Check dough by gently pressing a fingertip into the dough. If the shape of your fingertip remains, the dough is ready.
7. Press dough to flatten out air bubbles.
8. Add a little more flour to the cutting board or wax paper.
9. Turn dough from bowl onto lightly floured surface. Knead dough a few times.
10. Divide dough in half and shape each half into a ball. Let dough rest 10 minutes.
11. Meanwhile, grease loaf pans, using one tablespoon butter or margarine for each.
12. Press each ball of dough flat, then roll tightly into a tube about as long as the bread pan. Tuck ends under.
13. Place shaped dough in pans with the smooth side up.
14. Cover loaves with towel. Let rise about 45 minutes or until doubled in size.
15. Press one of the loaves with fingertip. When shape of fingertip remains, loaves are ready to bake.
16. Heat oven to 375°F. Bake loaves for 45 minutes or until golden brown. Remove bread from pans and cool on wire racks.

Makes 2 loaves

Water along the Oregon Trail

On the Oregon Trail, emigrants filled water barrels at rivers, streams, and water holes. They saved the water for drinking and cooking. Emigrants needed to camp near water spots and refill water barrels at least every second day.

For the most part, emigrant trains were within a few miles of water at all times. The trails west followed and crossed the Platte River, the North Platte River, the Sweetwater River, the Green, Bear, and Snake Rivers, as well as many others along the routes. Which rivers overlanders crossed depended on whether they were headed for California, Oregon, or Utah.

Some river water was muddy and tasted terrible. But overlanders drank the water because they had no other choice. They often strained the water through a cloth to filter out some of the sand. Many emigrants complained in their diaries about the taste of the water. One emigrant noted that the Platte River was not a river at all, but "simply moving sand."

Overlanders rarely drank plain water. They mixed the water with coffee or tea. Many emigrants carried along lemon extract or lemon syrup to mix with water. They sometimes added raspberry-flavored vinegar. Emigrants made the vinegar and flavored it with berries they picked along the way. They sometimes mixed the vinegar with the lemon extract or syrup to make lemonade.

Some rivers and water spots along the trail contained alkali. This acid mingled with the soil and entered the groundwater. Alkali water killed livestock.

16

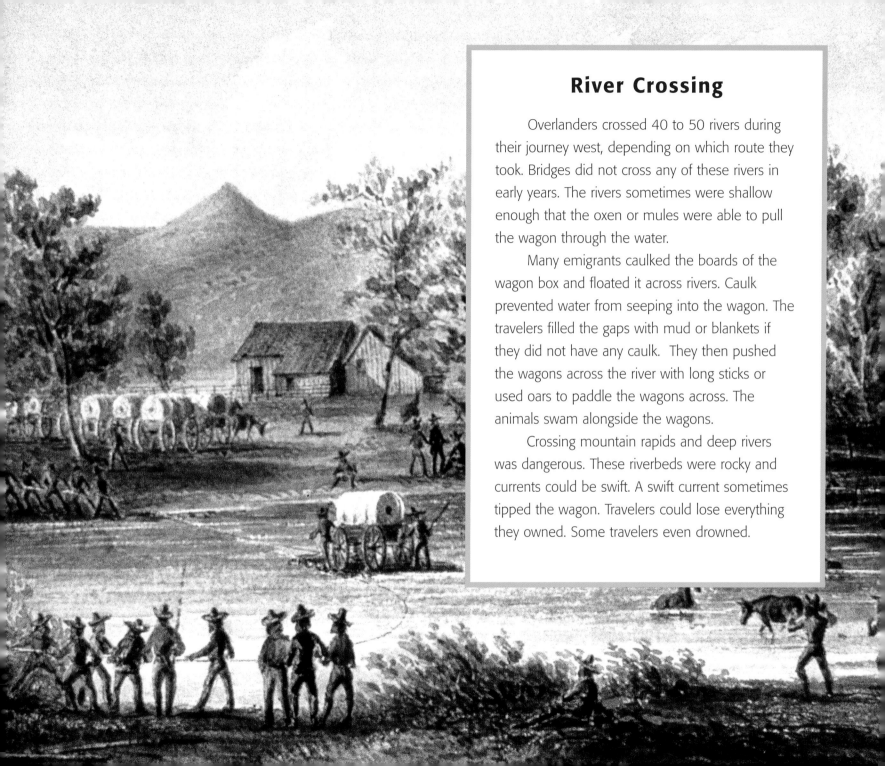

River Crossing

Overlanders crossed 40 to 50 rivers during their journey west, depending on which route they took. Bridges did not cross any of these rivers in early years. The rivers sometimes were shallow enough that the oxen or mules were able to pull the wagon through the water.

Many emigrants caulked the boards of the wagon box and floated it across rivers. Caulk prevented water from seeping into the wagon. The travelers filled the gaps with mud or blankets if they did not have any caulk. They then pushed the wagons across the river with long sticks or used oars to paddle the wagons across. The animals swam alongside the wagons.

Crossing mountain rapids and deep rivers was dangerous. These riverbeds were rocky and currents could be swift. A swift current sometimes tipped the wagon. Travelers could lose everything they owned. Some travelers even drowned.

Raspberry-Vinegar Lemonade

The raspberry vinegar for this recipe needs to sit a week before use.

For raspberry vinegar:

Ingredients
2 cups cider vinegar
2 cups fresh raspberries

Equipment
medium saucepan
liquid measuring cups
clean dish towel
2 small jars with plastic lids or
    plastic wrap to cover mouth
    of jars under a metal lid
fine wire-mesh strainer

For lemonade:

Ingredients
8 cups cold water or unflavored
    sparkling mineral water
1 cup sugar
½ cup raspberry vinegar
2 teaspoons lemon extract

Equipment
liquid measuring cup
wooden spoon
2-quart pitcher
dry-ingredient
    measuring cups
measuring spoons

To make raspberry vinegar:

1. Combine 2 cups vinegar and 2 cups raspberries in saucepan over medium-high heat. Bring to boil. Reduce heat to medium-low. Cook, uncovered, 3 minutes.
2. Remove pan from heat and let sit for several minutes.
3. Cover saucepan with towel. Let mixture cool.
4. Pour mixture into jar. Cover tightly with plastic lid or cover with plastic wrap and then tightly seal with metal lid. Let stand in cool, dark place for 1 week.
5. Pour raspberry vinegar through strainer into second jar. Discard fruit.
6. Store in a cool, dark place. Keeps for up to 6 months.

Makes 2 cups raspberry vinegar

To make lemonade:

Combine 8 cups cold water, 1 cup sugar, ½ cup raspberry vinegar, and 2 teaspoons lemon extract in pitcher. Stir well.

Use leftover raspberry vinegar for salad dressings or to sprinkle on cooked greens or beans.

Makes 6 to 8 servings

The Donner Tragedy

Traveling across the mountains and plains was difficult, and most emigrants were eager to find a quicker, easier route. A group of emigrants called the Donner Party were in search of a quick way to the California territory in 1846.

A westward guidebook, written by Lansford Hastings, advertised a shortcut to the California Territory through the Wasatch Mountains and across the Salt Lake Desert. The guide claimed that the shortcut would save 350 miles (563 kilometers), although it had never been tested. The Donner Party wanted to attempt the shortcut. They separated from their wagon train and headed into the Wasatch Mountains.

The rough land slowed the Donner Party. The three-day journey across the Wasatch Mountains turned into 12 days. Supplies were running low, and the Donner Party still had to cross the Salt Lake Desert. By the time the group made it to the main trail, they were a full three weeks behind the original wagon train. They were tired, out of food, and many of their animals had died in the desert. Some members rode to Sutter's Fort for supplies while the remainder of the party rested for a week. Hastings' guidebook warned readers that a difficult mountain range lay ahead.

The Donner Party started into the Sierra Nevada Mountain Range in October. Winter came early, and the emigrants were stranded in a blizzard. They built shelters and waited for help. The first rescue party arrived more than six months later. Many of the emigrants had already died of starvation. Other members had to choose between death from starvation and eating those who had died. Less than half of the Donner Party survived the ordeal.

A Journey of Danger and Hardship

The greatest cause of death on the Oregon Trail was disease. Most people died of cholera. Emigrants became sick with cholera after drinking polluted water. They experienced vomiting, diarrhea, and dehydration. Within a day, the sick person often died.

Travelers who did not bring dried fruit along on the trip were in danger of getting scurvy. Scurvy is a disease that is caused by a lack of Vitamin C. Emigrants counted on fruits and vegetables for their supply of Vitamin C. On the Oregon Trail, finding these foods was difficult. Emigrants picked dandelion greens, chard, spinach, and berries to keep from getting scurvy.

Accidents occurred throughout the journey. Some travelers slipped while getting in and out of their wagons. Wagon wheels often crushed or injured these emigrants, who were mostly young children. Accidental gunfire injured or killed some emigrants. Guns did not have safety devices and sometimes fired when overlanders removed them from the wagon or loaded them.

Overlanders lived through daily discomforts. Prairie winds blew dust into emigrants' eyes, noses, and mouths. The hot sun made them tired and thirsty. Many travelers did not bathe or change clothes regularly. They lived with dirty, smelly clothes for many days. These unsanitary conditions caused many emigrants to become infested with head and body lice.

Fierce storms made travel difficult for emigrants. Large hailstones and strong winds damaged wagons and killed livestock. Lightning sometimes struck an emigrant or started a prairie fire. Wagons often sunk into muddy trails and slowed travel. If wagons became stuck too deeply in the mud, emigrants had to shovel out the wheels.

Cooked Greens with Bacon and Vinegar

Ingredients

10 cups fresh greens
  (spinach, mustard greens,
  Swiss chard)
5 slices bacon
1 tablespoon vinegar or
  raspberry vinegar

Equipment

dry-ingredient measuring cups
large bowl
cutting board
sharp knife
Dutch oven or large saucepan
spatula
paper towel
clean coffee can
measuring spoons

Wagon train members circled their wagons at night to protect the livestock from wolves and to keep the animals from straying.

1. Wash greens. Remove any tough stems.
2. Tear greens into medium-sized pieces. Toss together in bowl.
3. Cut bacon into 1-inch (2.5-centimeter) pieces.
4. In Dutch oven or saucepan, cook bacon until crisp. Place bacon on paper towel to cool.
5. Pour bacon fat into coffee can. Scoop 2 tablespoons of bacon fat into Dutch oven or saucepan.
6. Add greens to Dutch oven or saucepan. Cook over medium heat 6 to 8 minutes or until the greens have wilted and are tender.
7. Sprinkle with bacon pieces and 1 tablespoon vinegar. Use raspberry vinegar if you like. Serve immediately.

Makes 6 servings

Fort Laramie

Emigrants welcomed the sight of Fort Laramie in Wyoming. The trip was one-third completed when travelers reached this point. The trading post, which became a U.S. Army fort in 1849, was a main stop along the Oregon Trail. Emigrants purchased supplies and repaired their wagons. They took the opportunity to buy milk, eggs, and other fresh products. Many travelers had not tasted these items for weeks.

Supplies at Fort Laramie were expensive. Traders knew that travelers would be desperate for food and supplies at this point. Emigrants paid the high prices because they had no other choice. Many emigrants had brought cherished items to sell at the fort. If the traders did not buy their belongings, travelers dumped items on the way out of Fort Laramie. The oxen and mules would not be able to haul heavy loads over the Rocky Mountains. The remainder of the journey was the most difficult.

Oxen, mules, and horses also were available at Fort Laramie. If their livestock had become sick or weak, emigrants could trade them for healthy animals. The weak animals rested at Fort Laramie and later were sold to other emigrants. Healthy animals could be bought at a high price. Emigrants who did not purchase healthy animals rested their livestock for several days.

Some overlanders were tired of traveling by the time they reached the fort. They thought that the land out west was not worth the hardships endured on the trail. Sick and discouraged emigrants stayed at Fort Laramie until they regained their strength. They then resupplied their wagons and returned east.

Strawberry Ice Cream

Ingredients
1 pint fresh strawberries
1½ cups whipping cream
½ cup sugar
⅛ teaspoon salt
1 cup canning salt
5 pounds (2.5 kilograms) crushed ice

Equipment
strainer
cutting board
sharp knife
food processor or blender
liquid measuring cup
dry-ingredient measuring cups
measuring spoons
1-pound (.5-kilogram) clean coffee can with lid
1½ -to 2-pound (.7- to .9-kilogram) clean coffee can with lid
duct tape
dish towel

1. Rinse strawberries in strainer.
2. Carefully cut green leaves from strawberries and cut strawberries in half.
3. In food processor or blender, blend berries until smooth.
4. Add 1½ cups whipping cream, ½ cup sugar, and ⅛ teaspoon salt. Blend until smooth.
5. Pour mixture into the smaller coffee can. Seal with plastic lid. Tape around side of lid to can with duct tape to prevent leaking.
6. Spread 2-inch (5-centimeter) layer of crushed ice in the larger coffee can.
7. Set coffee can with strawberry mixture in middle of larger can. Sprinkle 2 tablespoons of canning salt on top of ice around smaller can.
8. Pack with ice to up to half the height of smaller can. Sprinkle ice with ¼ cup canning salt.
9. Pack with ice to top of larger can. Sprinkle with 2 tablespoons canning salt. Place lid on larger coffee can and seal with duct tape to prevent leaking.
10. Lay towel down on a counter top or table.
11. Place can on towel and roll back and forth slowly for about 5 minutes.
12. Carefully remove duct tape and lid from larger can.
13. Pack ice to the top and sprinkle with 2 tablespoons salt. Replace lid and duct tape.
14. Repeat steps 11 through 13 three more times or until cream mixture has hardened.
15. Spoon into bowls and eat. Leftover ice cream can be frozen.

When overlanders saw Chimney Rock, they knew Fort Laramie was near. Most emigrants wrote about this massive formation in their journals or diaries. Chimney Rock measures 325 feet (99 meters) high from the base.

Celebrations and Ceremonies

Emigrants traveling the Oregon Trail took time from their journey to celebrate special occasions. Independence Day was an important holiday for emigrants. Most travelers hoped to reach a landmark known as Independence Rock by the Fourth of July. If they arrived at this large hill of granite by early July, they knew the wagon train was on schedule.

Overlanders saved special foods purchased at Fort Laramie for the Independence Day celebration. They baked pies and fresh bread. Children made lemonade by adding sugar, citric acid, and a few drops of essence of lemon to their water. Women sewed American flags with scraps of fabric. Some emigrants danced around the campfire while others carved or painted their names onto the surface of Independence Rock. Some of the names still can be seen today.

The travelers also took time for wedding ceremonies. Young couples often met during their journey. Wagon train members sometimes shot guns, banged kettles, and shook the couple's wagon late into the wedding night. This celebration was called a chivaree.

Some nights, emigrants played cards or dice. Many overlanders brought musical instruments such as fiddles and banjos along on the trip. At night, travelers gathered around the fire to sing and dance.

Independence Rock was one of the most noted of all landmarks in emigrant diaries. The rock stands 128 feet (39 meters) tall, 700 feet (213 meters) wide, and 1,900 feet (579 meters) long.

Dried Apple Dumplings

Ingredients

Apple layer:

1 8-ounce package dried apples or dried mixed fruit

7 cups water

¾ cup firmly packed brown sugar

1 teaspoon cinnamon

½ teaspoon ginger

1 tablespoon lemon juice

Dumplings:

1 cup all-purpose flour

¼ cup cornmeal

¼ cup sugar

2 teaspoons baking powder

1 egg

¼ cup water

Equipment

large cutting board

sharp knife

medium saucepan

liquid measuring cup

dry-ingredient measuring cups

measuring spoons

wooden spoon

medium bowl

small bowl

hand mixer

spoon

To make apple layer:

1. Chop apples into small pieces.
2. In saucepan, combine apples, 7 cups water, ¾ cup brown sugar, 1 teaspoon cinnamon, and ½ teaspoon ginger. Bring the mixture to a boil.
3. Reduce heat to medium and simmer for 25 minutes. (Prepare dumplings while mixture simmers.)
4. Add 1 tablespoon lemon juice. Cook 5 minutes.
5. Remove cover from apple mixture. Gently drop spoonfuls of dumpling mixture onto simmering apple mixture. Make sure the dumplings sit on the top of the apple layer and do not sink.
6. Cover tightly. Cook over medium-low heat for 15 minutes. Do not remove cover during cooking.

To make dumplings:

1. In medium bowl, combine 1 cup flour, ¼ cup cornmeal, ¼ cup sugar, 2 teaspoons baking powder, and ½ teaspoon salt.
2. In small bowl, beat together 1 egg and ¼ cup water with hand mixer.
3. Add egg mixture to flour mixture. Mix with spoon just until all ingredients are moistened. Do not overstir or dumplings will be tough. To serve, spoon apple mixture into bowls. Top with dumplings.

Makes 6 servings

Rocky Mountain Challenges

The Rocky Mountains were a challenge to cross for both travelers and animals. Emigrants struggled to bring wagons across the rough land. Oxen had to pull the heavy wagons up steep slopes. The high altitudes made many of the animals sick and weak.

Wagons did not have brakes. They could speed out of control and crash if they rolled downhill too fast. Some emigrants lost their wagons and even their lives this way. They often secured ropes through the spokes of the wagon wheels. With the wagon wheels locked, the wagons moved more slowly downhill.

In the Rocky Mountains, emigrants had to adjust their food preparation for the higher altitudes. Water boils at a lower temperature in high places, and food takes longer to cook. This cooking difference puzzled many emigrants who were not used to mountain cooking.

Travelers rationed out their food in the hope that it would last throughout the mountain journey. They divided the food for the number of days they expected to travel and tried to eat limited amounts. Once emigrants reached Idaho and eastern Oregon, they traded with American Indians for salmon and other foods.

Beans and Rice

Many overlanders ate beans and rice during the last part of the journey. These dried foods had not spoiled during the months on the Oregon Trail.

Ingredients
1 tablespoon vegetable oil
1 small onion
¾ cup long-grain rice, uncooked
1½ cups water
½ teaspoon dried thyme
½ teaspoon salt
¼ teaspoon black pepper
⅛ teaspoon red (cayenne) pepper
1 can (16 ounces) cooked light-red
   kidney beans

Equipment
Dutch oven or large saucepan with lid
measuring spoons
sharp knife
cutting board
spatula
dry-ingredient measuring cups
wooden spoon
liquid measuring cup
colander

---

1. Heat 1 tablespoon oil in Dutch oven or large saucepan over medium-high heat.
2. Remove skin from onion. Chop onion.
3. Cook onion in oil until tender, turning occasionally.
4. Stir in ¾ cup rice. Cook 2 minutes, stirring frequently.
5. Add 1½ cups water, ½ teaspoon thyme, ½ teaspoon salt, ¼ teaspoon pepper, and ⅛ teaspoon red pepper. Red pepper is spicy. If you do not like spicy food, you may wish to add just a pinch between your thumb and forefinger.
6. Reduce heat to low. Cover. Cook 25 minutes or until all liquid is absorbed.
7. Gently stir in beans.

Overlanders sometimes took apart their wagons to lower them down steep hills.

Makes 6 to 8 servings

A New Life in the West

Emigrants who survived the journey arrived in Oregon, California, or Utah in the fall. They had hard work to do before winter. Some settlers cut down trees and built log cabins. Others made their homes from sod. They cut blocks of soil and grass and stacked them to build houses. The settlers cleared land for farming. Some set up businesses in newly built towns.

Few stores were available where pioneers could purchase food or household items. Early settlers sold fruits and vegetables to the emigrants. Some women had saved seeds during the journey and planted gardens right away. Others had to use the seeds from the fruits and vegetables they bought.

Many emigrants struggled through the first years in their new home. Overlanders often started the trip with farm animals. But most of the cows and chickens died on the Oregon Trail. Some travelers ate the surviving animals when they ran out of food.

Because food choices were limited, settlers could not be picky about what they ate. Many people lived through the first years by hunting and fishing. If they shot rabbits every day, they ate rabbits every day. Some settlers made carrots into jam if there was no fruit. Settlers continued to cook their food over a fire until they could afford to buy a stove.

Many overlanders were eager to build new homes and towns in the West. The hard work and dedication of the emigrants brought settlement to this area of the United States.

Emigrants built homes and cleared land for farming after their long journey west.

Oregon Venison Stew

Settlers of the West survived on wild game during their first years. Wild meat often was stewed with vegetables. Emigrants hunted rabbits, raccoons, squirrels, and deer. The meat from deer is called venison.

Ingredients

1 large onion
2 pounds venison or stew beef
1 tablespoon vegetable oil
4 cups water
3 beef bouillon cubes
1 1/2 teaspoons dried marjoram
1/8 teaspoon salt

1/8 teaspoon pepper
2 medium carrots
1 medium parsnip
1 medium potato
1 cup chopped cabbage
1/3 cup all-purpose flour
1/3 cup water

Equipment

sharp knife
cutting board
Dutch oven or large saucepan
wooden spoon
liquid measuring cup
measuring spoons
vegetable peeler
dry-ingredient measuring cups
small bowl

1. Remove skin from onion. Chop into small pieces.
2. Cut meat into 1-inch (2.5-centimeter) chunks.
3. Heat oil in Dutch oven or large saucepan over medium-high heat.
4. Cook meat and onions in oil until meat is browned, stirring occasionally.
5. Stir in 4 cups water, 3 bouillon cubes, 1 1/2 teaspoons marjoram, 1/8 teaspoon salt and 1/8 teaspoon pepper. Cook 40 minutes over low heat, partially covered.

While mixture cooks:

6. Peel and slice 2 carrots, 1/2 inch (1.3 centimeters) thick.
7. Peel parsnip. Chop into small pieces.
8. Cut potato into 3/4-inch (1.9-centimeter) cubes.
9. Chop cabbage.
10. Stir in carrots, parsnip, potato, and 1 cup cabbage. Cook 1 hour or until meat and vegetables are tender.
11. In bowl, mix 1/3 cup flour and 1/3 cup water until smooth. Stir into stew.
12. Cook stew 5 minutes or until thickened, stirring occasionally.

Makes 7 to 8 servings

Words to Know

altitude (AL-ti-tood)—the height of land or an object above the ground; cooking times differed in the high altitudes of the Rocky Mountains.

butter churn (BUHT-ur CHURN)—a tall, narrow, wooden or stone crock containing a long, paddled stick and fitted with a lid; a person poured cream into the crock and moved the stick in circles and up and down until the cream thickened into butter.

caulk (KAWK)—a waterproof paste that is applied to cracks and edges that need to be watertight; some emigrants used caulk to seal the wagon box during river crossing.

emigrant (EM-uh-grehnt)—a person who travels from a home country or location to another; emigrants moved from their homes in the East to settle in the West.

hail stones (HAYL STONES)—moisture that forms into packed ice and falls from the sky instead of rain or snow; hail can range in size from pea-size to the size of a softball.

territory (TER-uh-tor-ee)—an area of the United States that is not yet a state

wagon train (WAG-uhn TRANE)—a group of wagons traveling together for protection and help on the trails west

To Learn More

Erickson, Paul. *Daily Life in a Covered Wagon.* New York: Puffin Books, 1997.

Hester, Sallie. *A Covered Wagon Girl: The Diary of Sally Hester, 1849-1850.* Edited by Christy Steele with Ann Hodgson. Diaries, Letters, and Memoirs. Mankato, Minn.: Blue Earth Books, 2000.

Kalman, Bobbie. *The Wagon Train.* Life in the Old West. New York: Crabtree Publishing, 1999.

King, David C. *Pioneer Days: Discover the Past with Fun Projects, Games, Activities, and Recipes.* American Kids in History Series. New York: John Wiley and Sons, Inc., 1997.

Places to Write and Visit

Chimney Rock National Historic Site
P.O. Box F
Bayard, NE 69334-0680

End of the Oregon Trail Interpretive Center
1726 Washington Street
Oregon City, OR 97045

Fort Laramie National Historic Site
P.O. Box 86
Fort Laramie, WY 82212

National Historic Oregon Trail Interpretive Center at Flagstaff Hill
Oregon Highway 86
Baker City, OR 97814-0987

The National Oregon/California Trail Center
322 North Fourth Street
Montpelier, ID 83254

Scotts Bluff National Monument
P.O. Box 27
Gering, NE 69341-0027

Internet Sites

Emigrant Road
http://www.emigrantroad.com

End of the Oregon Trail
http://endoftheoregontrail.org

The Oregon-California Trails Association
http://www.OCTA-trails.org

Oregon Trail Adventure
http://www.proaxis.com/~olsenk

Oregon Trail Time Frame
http://www.geocities.com/Athens/Ithaca/5531

Index